FAQ

TEEN LIFE™

FREQUENTLY ASKED QUESTIONS ABOUT

Stuttering

Frances O'Connor

ROSEN
PUBLISHING®

New York

Published in 2008 by The Rosen Publishing Group, Inc.
29 East 21st Street, New York, NY 10010

Library of Congress Cataloging-in-Publication Data

O'Connor, Frances.
Frequently asked questions about stuttering / Frances O'Connor.—
1st ed.
     p.cm.—(FAQ: Teen Life)
Includes bibliographical references and index.
ISBN-13: 978-1-4042-1931-1
ISBN-10: 1-4042-1931-5
1. Stuttering in adolescence—Juvenile literature.
I. Title.
RJ496.S8O26 2007
618.92'8554—dc22

                                                                200700102

Manufactured in the United States of America

contents

Introduction

For many people, stuttering is a fact of life. In fact, more than five million American children and teenagers stutter, as do more than three million adults. After early childhood, people are diagnosed with stuttering when they have a tendency to repeat or prolong sounds, or have trouble making clear sounds. No matter the severity of one's stuttering condition, however, all speech impediments can be improved so that speaking is much easier and clearer.

According to the American Speech-Language-Hearing Association (ASHA), stuttering is "a communication disorder that affects the fluency of speech." Stuttering begins during childhood and, in some cases, persists throughout the person's life. The disorder is characterized by disruptions in the production of speech sounds. Speech-language pathologists refer to these disruptions as disfluencies. Most speakers produce brief disfluencies in speech from time to time. For instance, some words are repeated and others are preceded by interjections such as "um." Disfluencies are not necessarily problematic; however, they can impede communication when a speaker produces too many of them or does not resolve them promptly.

The Stuttering Foundation of America defines stuttering as "a communication disorder in which the flow of speech is broken by repetitions (li-li-like this), prolongations (lllllike

In preschool, stuttering affects more boys than girls; for every girl who stutters at this stage, about two boys are affected.

this), or abnormal stoppages (no sound) of sounds and syllables. There may also be unusual facial and body movements associated with the effort to speak."

Even though everyone tends to pause when speaking, people who stutter get caught in longer pauses or have trouble making the sounds to get their message across clearly. According to ASHA, " Whatever the traits are, they obviously impair the individual's ability to string together the various muscle movements that are necessary to produce sentences fluently." Scientists have yet to determine the exact cause of stuttering, but they do have some clues. According to the

Stuttering Foundation of America, the four factors that contribute to the development of stuttering include:

▶ **Genetics** Approximately 60 percent of those who stutter have a family member who does also.
▶ **Child development** Kids with other speech and language problems are likely to stutter.
▶ **Neurophysiology** People who stutter process speech and language differently than other people.
▶ **Family dynamics** High expectations and fast-paced life-styles can contribute to stuttering.

Most children and some teenagers and adults stutter at some times in their lives. They repeat sounds or parts of words, and their disruptions do not need to be treated with the help of a speech therapist; the stutter goes away by itself. These people stutter occasionally and are not thought of as stutterers. Although about 5 percent of children are diagnosed with stuttering problems between the ages of two and six years, only 20 percent of those children will also stutter as adults according to David Lavid, M.D., author of *Understanding Stuttering*.

Most stuttering is diagnosed during childhood. According to the Stuttering Foundation of America, children between the ages of two and five may stutter frequently because they're learning how to speak in full sentences. Their stuttering is typical, and it usually ends after age five. If children continue stuttering beyond this age, or to a great degree as they learn to talk, they may need the help of a speech therapist to learn patterns of fluent speech. They will also benefit from speech therapy if they stumble over words, prolong sounds that form parts of a word, or repeat the same word several times before finishing a sentence. Usually a child's stuttering is diagnosed by a teacher, parent, or doctor by the time he or she is age seven. If a stuttering problem is not detected and treated during childhood, then the child will likely stutter as a teen.

one

WHAT ARE THE TYPES OF STUTTERING AND ITS TRIGGERS?

Speech disfluencies, or disruptions, are not the same as stuttering. Even though disfluencies can come and go in one's speech like stuttering, they are more infrequent. Speech disfluencies are usually marked by the occasional adding of "um," "uh," or "er" to fill a sentence or pause in the middle of a statement. They are repetitions of syllables or sounds that happen only sometimes, usually when the speaker is tired, angry, or stressed.

Stuttering is a more obvious, frequent speech pattern. It usually consists of repetition of the beginning of a word, like p-p-p-p-pencil, or the prolonging of a sound to get through a word, like Ffffffffffebruary. People who stutter have difficulty with their breathing and they often breathe improperly to produce clear sounds. A stutterer's breathing is often uneven, and he or she breathes in the midst of speaking,

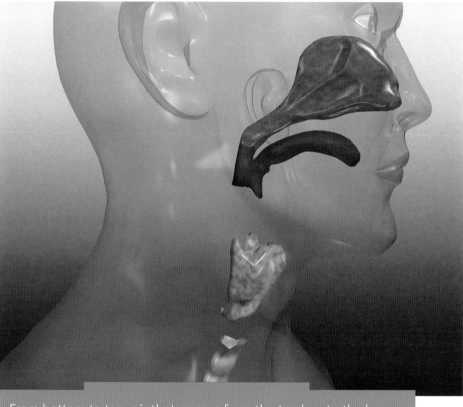

From bottom to top, air that passes from the trachea to the larynx, which contains the vocal cords, and the pharynx, is formed into speech sounds by the palate, tongue, and lips.

often when he or she is already in the middle of a sentence. Stutterers' voices may also rise in pitch or volume as they struggle to make themselves heard. To compensate for their condition, stutterers may also switch to different, less difficult-to-pronounce words when they begin speaking, or repeat sounds at different points during one sentence. Two common speech patterns stutterers have include:

➤ Blocking—Trying to make a sound and the flow of air stops completely in your larynx, tongue, or lips

➤ Repetition—Repeating one sound (b-b-b-boy), syllable (but-but-but-butter), word (Dan-Dan-Dan has the basketball) or phrase (in the-in the-in the hall)

Mild Stuttering

Mild stuttering resembles disrupted speech, but it happens more often. People who have mild stuttering problems are different from people who experience occasional speech disruption because mild stuttering can be more noticeable. When someone who has an occasional speech disruption is tired and slips on a word, he or she can easily laugh it off. Stutterers, on the other hand, often get caught on different parts of a sentence, such as "Aaaare there any a-a-a-a-ples lllleft?" It appears as if their words get stuck in their mouths or throats even before they become words, when they are still air coming up from the throat. Stuttering can involve a blocked airflow, which means that no air comes into the throat for a few seconds. This experience can be scary for stutterers, who are struggling to be heard. This block in airflow can be so extreme that stutterers trying to make sounds might get red in the face, blink a lot, or make awkward gestures.

Moderate Stuttering

Moderate stuttering is more severe and occurs more often than mild stuttering, but it involves all the characteristic airflow stoppages, repetition of sounds, and prolonging of sounds, and it is more noticeable. Moderate stutterers are aware that they have a problem, and they struggle more to make their speech clear. People who have moderate stuttering problems will often be red in the face, appear short of breath, and will blink a lot in frustration. They will often have contorted facial expressions due to the fact that they are working so hard to express themselves.

Severe Stuttering

People who are severe stutterers (also called confirmed stutterers) are unmistakably people who struggle to make clear sounds and statements. They must work very hard to speak and may avoid trying to speak aloud or in front of groups. They usually experience disfluency or disruption in many parts of each sentence and have very obvious signs of struggle—a red face, distorted mouth muscles, blinking, and a voice that's higher in pitch or louder than others. Severe stutters struggle with coherent speech every day, but not when they're singing or when they're with people whom they feel very comfortable or familiar with.

The Language Center

To understand stuttering and disrupted speech, you first have to understand how sounds are produced. Our brains are complicated storage units and machines that constantly store and produce language. Stuttering starts with the brain's language center, in the left cerebral hemisphere. The language center controls

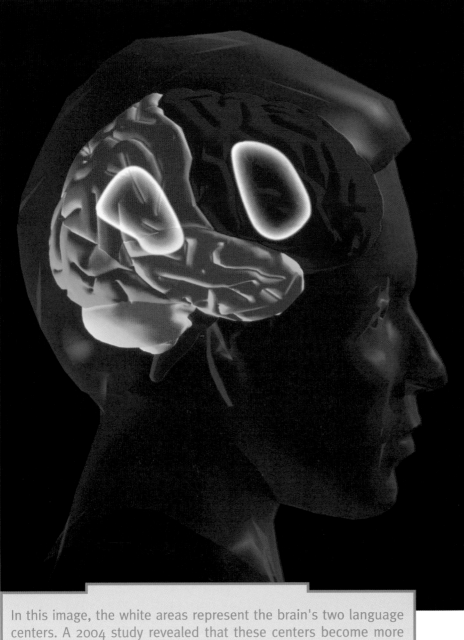

In this image, the white areas represent the brain's two language centers. A 2004 study revealed that these centers become more evenly distributed between the left and right hemispheres with age.

language—how you learn new words, where you store vocabulary words, how you put sentences together, and how you think about language. According to researchers, scientists have noticed unusual electrical activity between the right and left halves of the brain in people who stutter. The left hemisphere of the brain shows less than normal activity when someone stutters, and the right hemisphere shows more than normal activity. Scientists remain unsure of what this difference in electrical activity means and exactly how it influences how people who stutter form thoughts or words.

How Speech Is Formed

What we do know is that once the brain needs to tell the body to produce a sound in order to ask a question or say hello to a friend, it sends electrical signals, or impulses, to other parts of the body. The body parts responsible for producing sounds must spring into action to work together in a quick-moving chain of events, starting with breathing. After you breathe in, you breathe out, which is the first step to making a sound. As the breath flows up on its way out of the body, it gets pushed out by the diaphragm, a thick layer of muscle that is just below the lungs and helps to facilitate breathing. The air then moves through your trachea, or windpipe, into your throat, where it goes through the vocal cords in your larynx (voice box). You then make the sound you want. After the vocal cords have opened and closed around the sound you've made, the sound passes over your soft palate (the soft part of the roof of your mouth), then over your hard palate (the hard part of the roof of your

Ten Great Questions to Ask Your Doctor or Speech Therapist

1 How often do I need to see you to practice/improve my speech?

2 Can I still speak in public and act in the school plays?

3 Do I need to practice certain sounds or sentences?

4 What should I do if I start stuttering when reading aloud?

5 What do I do if I start stuttering around my friends and teammates?

6 What's causing my speech difficulties?

7 What advice can I give my friends to help me when I can't get a word out?

8 What can I ask my teacher to do to help me when I'm at school?

9 Can you help me learn to be less nervous when I stutter in any situation?

10 Since I stutter, will my children stutter?

mouth behind your top front teeth). The sound is guided by your tongue, which hits the top of your mouth and back of your teeth. At the same time, you move your jaw up and down and your lips open and close around a sound, making it clear. When someone stutters, he or she experiences distortions of the muscles in the jaw, vocal cords, tongue, lips, and soft palate. The muscles of a stuttering person don't tighten (contract) and loosen (expand) in the way they should around a sound. They often contract too much or too often, or stay loose at the wrong times, making it difficult for a stutterer's words to be clear.

It's very important to remember that stuttering is not a psychological or emotional problem. Although the brain controls speech and language, people who stutter are just as intelligent as nonstutterers are. Stuttering is not a mental illness.

At first glance, mild stuttering and normal speech disfluencies, which are both accompanied by awkward gestures and facial expressions, are sometimes hard to tell apart.

Environments Influence Stuttering

The most common trigger for stuttering is a negative environment. If a person who stutters lives with parents, siblings, or other family members who speak in a rush at the dinner table and talk over one another, the stutterer feels forced to do the same, out of the fear that no one will listen to him if he talks more slowly. This can make a person's stuttering worse. Also, if a stutterer is around family members or friends who try to finish his sentences for him as he struggles, it is more frustrating than being allowed to finish his own thoughts. The same goes for being hurried through a sentence. If people tell a person who stutters to speak faster, it also hinders his ability to speak fluently.

If a child who stutters was ridiculed by parents, teachers, students, or siblings and told to "just spit it out" or to "stop playing games" when he was experiencing a speech problem, his stuttering problem can become more long-lasting or require more extensive speech therapy. Being teased as a child can make a person who stutters experience disfluent speech for longer than a child whose stuttering was recognized early and was made to feel OK about it.

Self-Esteem

A person's own feelings about himself or herself also affect how bad a stuttering situation can be. If you are a stutterer and feel very self-conscious all the time, you might be overthinking most speaking situations. Except when speaking in front of an auditorium, people listening aren't hanging on your every word or sound in most situations such as in class, at the supermarket, or in a restaurant. They're probably focused on their part of the job, like taking your order properly or helping you find what you're looking for, or they are thinking about their next steps, such as whether or not they should offer you something else or counting your change properly. Even when addressing a large group of people, it's not uncommon for your listeners to be thinking about what they had for lunch, when their homework assignments are due, or what their mom told them last night. When they tune in

One study reports that children who stutter are teased 35 percent more than nonstutterers. The most common form of teasing is imitation, when peers mock the way the stutterer speaks.

to listen to your message, they are listening to what you're saying, not how you say it. Everyone has different accents and ways of expressing themselves, and your audience won't be looking at you silently waiting for you to mispronounce something or stumble over a word. As a stutterer, it's important to talk about your emotions about speaking to other people with your parents and speech therapist without letting anxiety take over.

Certain life situations also tend to make it harder for someone who stutters to speak clearly. Timed situations such as answering the phone or leaving a message on voice mail frequently make

To improve phone speaking skills, stutterers should observe and listen to nonstutterers on the phone, especially when they hesitate to speak or experience a lack of fluency.

stutterers feel pressured; they know they have a very short period of time in which to produce a sound perfectly. Speaking in front of a group makes most speakers nervous, and it's especially true for a person who stutters. Stutterers will find that having practice sessions with a speech therapist where they pretend they're in these situations will make the real moments less intense.

two

HOW DO I LIVE WITH STUTTERING?

If you stutter, you will become the successful person you were meant to be by overcoming your speech disfluencies or disruptions with the help of a network of people. In your network are your classmates, family, and friends. You may face some of your most difficult challenges in the places you share with these people—the classroom and your home. However, if you understand these relationships well, and ask the people in your network to work with you, together you will face the challenges of the future armed with more self-confidence and the ability to speak to anyone, anywhere, at any time and under any circumstances.

Parents and Siblings

If you stutter, remember that your parents and siblings are not responsible for making you a stutterer, even if one of them stutters. You didn't "catch" stuttering by listening to them speak, and they weren't mean to you when you were a child to make you into a person who stutters. Scientists understand enough from their studies of parents of children who stutter to know that stuttering is not the result of psychological damage parents do to their kids. While stuttering may be a family trait, your parents didn't mold you into having disfluent speech. It is important to remind your family that there are ways in which they can help you improve your speaking.

The Stuttering Foundation of America publishes a list of things that families can do to help someone who stutters, and you may want to pass this list onto your parents, or post the list in your house for everyone to read.

Solutions That Can Help Reduce Stuttering

●➤ Seek a calmer lifestyle
●➤ Speak less hurriedly
●➤ Finish your thoughts
●➤ Do not rush to finish speaking
●➤ Pause a second or so before responding to questions
●➤ Turn off the television and radio during conversations

You can also talk to your parents and siblings about how your speech therapy is progressing. Tell them about what you are working on, what you're still finding difficult to pronounce, and situations that worry you. This is a way you can share your

Members of Our Time Theatre Company rehearse for the company's third annual benefit gala on April 11, 2005, in New York City. The company provides a theatrical outlet for young people who stutter.

feelings with your family, and they can express their support. You may not immediately notice the positive changes in your speech, but your family likely will. They spend the most time around you and can give you the boost you'll need to do well in situations in the outside world.

Speaking in Class

Speaking in class is a stressful situation for most students in middle and high school, not just students who stutter. The best way to handle any uncomfortable situations is to discuss your

Turning off or minimizing distractions such as the television, radio, or cell phones during family gatherings or conversations can help family members who stutter engage more fully.

feelings with your teacher at the beginning of the year about your speech problems and what situations he or she can help you avoid. For example, it may be very difficult for you to have other students jump over you and finish your thoughts or shout that they disagree before you're finished speaking. If your teacher is planning to make debates a part of the class discussions, you can work together on situations that will allow you to participate without feeling intimidated.

Oral presentations are part of classroom activities, especially for teens. Even if you stutter, you shouldn't avoid these moments, especially since you can practice and prepare for them ahead of time. Explain to your teacher that you will need time to prepare, then work with your speech therapist to go over your speech or report. You can also practice what you are going to say in front of family members to try your hand at having an audience. It helps to deliver your thoughts to friendly faces in a rehearsal before the real event.

Classmates

Hopefully, your classmates are mature, kind people who are also respectful of people's differences. However, chances are they are experiencing the rapid life changes of the teen years and are trying to figure out who they are. Most teens feel worried about their changing bodies, voices, looks, and relationships. Teens frequently think that it's OK to put other people down as a way of making a joke or to make themselves feel better about their own insecurities. There are no excuses for being rude, but insensitive exchanges are typical between peers in a middle school and high school setting.

To guard against any joking around or comments that might make you feel bad, it's best to first believe in yourself. If you confidently explain to your classmates who may have made insensitive remarks about your stuttering that it is a speech pattern that you're working on and nothing to be ashamed of—which it isn't—they should have nothing to say. You may want to take the same approach you did with your teacher by explaining to classmates that you stutter before they hear you stutter. This will take away the fear of them finding out, and it's

When a stutterer raises her hand in class to speak, she's feeling confident. This is an ideal time for the teacher and other students to help her build her communication skills.

not a secret for you to worry about slipping because everyone will already know and understand that you might express yourself in speech patterns that are occasionally disrupted.

If classmates decide that it's OK to make fun of your speech, tell them that they are rude. Don't accept their bullying behavior, and do tell a teacher that it's happened. He or she can address the behavior policies of your school and classroom with your whole class without mentioning you by name, helping to stop behavior that is unfair and wrong.

Friends

Your close friends can improve your "safety zone" at school and help you get through situations that are difficult. Chances are, you already feel so comfortable around your friends that you hardly stutter around them, or if you do, they hardly notice it. If for some reason your stuttering is causing a tough spot between you and your friends, remind them that they can always talk about it with you. Stuttering shouldn't be the "elephant in the room" that everyone sees but feels scared to talk about. It may seem like it's not your job to make your friends feel comfortable because you're the one who is struggling with disrupted speech and the feelings of worry that sometimes come with it, but it's actually a proven cycle.

Dr. Hugo Gregory, professor and the head of the Speech and Language Pathology Department at Northwestern University (who is also a stutterer), wrote that he noticed in his first two years of college that "a stutterer has to take responsibility for making

Outside of school, your friends should not enable you to avoid speaking. For instance, they shouldn't get into the habit of talking to new people for you.

others feel comfortable in his presence." Once he became less sensitive to his own stuttering, the people around him became less uncomfortable. This in turn made him feel more at ease, and he stuttered less. He reversed the cycle of his own nervousness making other people more nervous by easing up a bit and remembering that true friends accept you for who you are.

Your friends should also respectfully follow the same rules mentioned before: They should not interrupt your speech in mid-sentence, insist that you speed your speech along, or finish sentences for you. If they forget this, gently remind them that this habit frustrates you. Explain also that although it might seem helpful, it will not help you get better at speaking more fluently or more quickly.

In addition, if new friends have "helpful suggestions" about fixing your speech that don't make any sense to you, don't hesitate to say that you're working with a speech therapist on the exact parts of your speech that are problematic. Gently explain to new people in your life about what kind of listening works best for you, and they will probably be able to work on this and leave the helpful hints up to your speech coach.

three

CAN I OVERCOME STUTTERING?

With practice, you can overcome the most difficult and embarrassing parts of your speech patterns and learn to become a fluent speaker. The first person whose help you should ask for is a speech therapist, or a speech pathologist. This is someone who might be on staff at your school or who your family doctor can recommend for further help. A speech therapist or pathologist is professionally educated in assessing, preventing, and treating speech disorders. He or she will have experience in understanding and treating the type of speech pattern that you have developed.

What Will the Speech Therapist Do?

The first thing a speech therapist will do is to speak with you in order to evaluate your speech patterns. This sounds

Many teens who stutter avoid social interactions and feel isolated, but meeting other young people who also stutter can help them feel comfortable enough to express themselves.

simple, but they are trained to listen for all different types of disfluencies. A good speech therapist should be able to identify exact problems in your speech patterns, such as where speech blocks are occurring and what words your muscles are having difficulty making clear.

After your initial evaluation, a speech therapist will begin to help you with exercises specific to your speech patterns. Don't be surprised if he or she starts by helping you say your name. As you might have experienced already, a lot of people who stutter struggle to introduce themselves. This is not because they have trouble remembering their names, but because it's usually the first thing they say to someone new. When we meet people, we want to make a good impression, and people who stutter often fear they'll sound silly in front of someone they don't know. It's this fear that makes them do the very thing they don't want to do—stutter or get blocked the moment they go to introduce themselves.

The speech therapist will work with you on practicing your speech but will also address the fears that may be contributing to the cause of your disfluent speech patterns. Often there are social triggers that make you very scared of rejection, of being ridiculed, or of not being heard or understood. A speech therapist can help you face your fears. Your therapist can guide you through handling these situations at the same time that he or she is teaching you how to form your words differently. This combined approach should help you build your confidence and speaking skills at the same time.

In case you are wondering about the types of speech exercises, they frequently consist of repeating the same sound or cluster of sounds, such as "th" words, or filling in sentences with a particular word or sound. Here are some common methods of correcting stuttering:

- **Self-correction:** Repeating the word that is causing you trouble
- **Gentle onset:** Beginning a difficult word softly
- **Blending:** A technique where you gradually shift from one part of a sound or syllable into the next
- **Carryover:** Practicing and maintaining your newly acquired speech skills in everyday social situations

The inventors of SpeechEasy listen to a speech-impaired man talk. SpeechEasy is worn in the ear and reduces stuttering by creating an echo for the stutterer to speak along with.

What Should You Do?

You will continually practice speech exercises until you become a successful, fluent speaker. The road to success is paved with many challenges, but with practice you can become part of the ranks of stutterers who lead perfectly typical, happy lives. By carrying the skills you learn in your sessions with a speech therapist to the other areas of your life, you will quickly pick up the habits of a fluent speaker who may stumble occasionally, but who is not afraid to try again.

You will grow to know yourself better and understand more fully which situations make you the most worried, but also those which make you comfortable. In knowing yourself, you will gain friendships with people who admire your self-confidence and have the same healthy respect for you as you do yourself.

How Stuttering Was Treated in the Past

According to author Benson Bobrick, author of the book *Knotted Tongues: Stuttering in History and the Quest for a Cure*, "stuttering is probably as old as speech itself." He states that ancient Egyptian records talk about stuttering, and so do poems from the ancient Chinese Han dynasty and a cuneiform tablet from ancient Mesopotamia dated AD 2500. Millions of people have struggled with and continue to struggle with speech disorders.

Bobrick also tells the story of Galen, a famous doctor who lived at the time of the Roman Empire. Galen thought that stuttering was caused by abnormal shape and dryness of the tongue. He considered his patients' ages and then decided if their tongues were too short, or too long, too wet, or too dry. He "cured" his patients by wrapping their tongues in little towels soaked in lettuce juice.

A long line of doctors after Galen also studied and tried to cure stuttering, some in especially creative ways. The doctor Cornelius Celsus, also a Roman who had lived during the empire, recommended that his patients chew mustard, garlic, and onions and massage their heads, necks, mouths, and chins.

Myths and Facts
About Stuttering

 Girls talk more than boys, so they tend to stutter more. Fact ➡ According to the Stuttering Foundation of America, there are three or four boys who stutter for every girl who does.

 People who stutter and have other speech disfluencies tend to be less smart than nonstutterers. Fact ➡ According to the Stuttering Foundation of America, people who stutter are just as smart as people who don't stutter.

 Stuttering is caused by emotional or psychological problems. Fact ➡ According to www.stutteringhelp.org, children and adults who stutter are no more likely to have psychological or emotional problems than children and adults who don't. There is no reason to believe that emotional trauma causes stuttering.

You can cure stuttering quickly by repeating a few sounds and words over a year's time. Fact ⟶ There is no "cure" for stuttering, but going to a speech therapist can help a stutterer work on becoming a more fluent speaker. Going to speech therapy can help people of all ages. While scientists are still researching drugs and electronic devices to aid fluent speech, this is not a miracle cure.

 People who stutter are better off taking jobs that don't deal with the public so that they don't have to talk too much. Fact ⟶ People who stutter can be successful at any job they wish—even one that involves talking to the whole world via radio or on television. Actors Samuel L. Jackson and James Earl Jones, scientist Isaac Newton, Oasis guitarist Noel Gallagher, President Theodore Roosevelt, politician Winston Churchill, actress Marilyn Monroe, authors John Updike and Lewis Carroll, and singer Carly Simon are people who dealt with their stuttering to become successful and famous.

His patients were then supposed to stick their heads in cold water and then vomit. He also started the practice of cutting the ligament under the tongue because he thought that this would loosen the tongue and liberate a person's speech.

In this 1984 photograph, a boy in the United Kingdom uses a video game program designed to help children with speech impediments use proper pronunciation.

Several doctors performed this ligament-cutting surgery ("frenectomy") on their patients throughout the centuries, but it didn't prove to cure patients. In the early 1300s, a lecturer in medicine, Bernard of Gordon, came very close to understanding what we know today about speech patterns. He described the way children sometimes stutter between the ages of two and four when they are learning to speak, and noted that the speech impediments usually went away.

In 1817, Jean Marc Gaspard Itard, a French doctor, thought that stuttering was caused by a weakness in the muscles of the tongue, and he recommended exercises for it. He also invented

On November 30, 2006, actor Samuel L. Jackson received the Bambi media prize in Stuttgart, Germany. Jackson overcame stuttering to become one of America's most successful actors.

a little fork made of ivory or gold to support a person's tongue while he or she was speaking; this fork was supposed to be worn inside the person's jaw.

These early efforts to understand and treat stuttering may sound strange. We are lucky that doctors and speech therapists today have the behavioral tools to diagnose and help people who develop a stutter or other speech disfluency. A speech therapist or speech pathologist at school or a local hospital can help you with language exercises to develop more fluent speech patterns.

four

HOW CAN I SHARPEN MY OTHER COMMUNICATION SKILLS?

When you communicate effectively, you are ensuring that your needs and point of view will be interpreted the way you intended. You are confirming that your message will be communicated clearly and with the desired result. You need to make sure that you are communicating with the appropriate person and in an appropriate way. If you can learn this very important skill, the quality of your life will improve. Whether at home, on the job, at school, or with friends, you will be happier and more successful in your relationships. Because of its obstacles, stuttering may sometimes make you feel like you're not as effective a communicator as others.

However, there are other ways people communicate with each other besides speaking that are important to

A handshake that comes with a firm grip and good eye contact can leave a powerful first impression on others that you are an outgoing and self-confident individual.

everyone. In fact, being able to communicate well using other forms of communication can be advantageous. This includes nonverbal communication, active listening, writing, and electronic communication. After all, when it comes down to it, it's not just what you have to say, but how you say it.

Nonverbal Communication

Our actions, posture, facial expressions, style of dress, and gaze all reveal things about us without words. People constantly send messages with their eyes, their smiles or frowns, and their body movements and posture. These are all examples of nonverbal communication.

Communicating nonverbally is often involuntary, meaning that it comes naturally, without thinking. We need to learn to be more aware of nonverbal signals (our own and other people's) and to use nonverbal communication to strengthen rather than to undermine our intended message. During a job interview, for example, the message you want to send is that you are capable, confident, alert, and ready to take on new responsibilities. If you do not look the interviewer in the eyes or if you give a weak, reluctant handshake, you may give the opposite impression. You must also be aware of your posture. Slouching over in your chair or leaning casually against a wall are both signs that you are not engaged by the conversation or situation at hand. Without realizing it, you could be sending the wrong message.

Effective nonverbal communication does not mean walking around with a fake grin on your face all the time. People will be able to tell that you are putting on an act. Instead of pretending, try to be more conscious of the attitudes and feelings you project and the effect that they are likely to have on others. Take notice of the ways in which you stand and sit, note if and when you use your hands to illustrate a point, and keep in mind what sort of messages you are projecting with your body when you are in a bad mood, or are angry or upset.

If your nonverbal messages are getting in the way of what you want to communicate, it is worth trying to change them. For example, if you slump in your chair with a vacant look on your face, you are sending the message that you don't care very much about what the person talking to you is saying. Rolling your eyes and sneering when you mention someone's name has the same effect as saying nasty things about him or her. If you fiddle with papers and avoid eye contact when talking to someone, you are telling him or her that you think that you do not need to pay close attention to what he or she is saying.

Even though we have all been taught not to judge a book by its cover, the way you dress and present yourself are also important forms of nonverbal communication. They can tell people to take you seriously—or on the other hand, not to bother, because you do not take yourself seriously. Your clothes and how you present yourself can also send the message that people should be intimidated by you. When there's a dress code or you're in a certain situation such as a formal dinner, your style of dress can tell people that you are sensitive to the nature of the environment or that you do not care enough to notice what is expected. In most cases, you will not have to give up your individual look; you might just have to fine-tune it a bit.

Active Listening

Besides communication in written, spoken, and nonverbal forms, communication also involves receiving messages through reading, listening, and interpreting other people's manner and behavior.

You may have always assumed that listening is a passive activity, since it usually involves just taking in information that the speaker communicates. But listening can be an activity in which you interact with the speaker and give positive feedback while receiving information at the same time. By practicing active listening habits, you will pay attention better and give the speaker the message that his or her words are being heard and understood.

One important aspect of active listening is making good eye contact. If you direct your gaze toward the person who is speaking, he or she will know that you are paying attention. If you are constantly looking around the room, the speaker will think that you do not care about what he or she is saying. If the speaker feels ignored, angered, or irritated by your lack of interest, it will be difficult for good communication to occur.

Responding to the speaker is another important component of active listening. Whether you simply nod your head or offer spoken feedback, an active response will show the speaker that

A good active listener sits appropriately close to the speaker and leans forward, which signals to the speaker that the listener is interested and paying close attention.

you are interested in what he or she is trying to communicate. One way to give feedback is to ask the speaker questions relating to what he or she is talking about. This demonstrates your interest and reinforces in your own mind the point that the speaker is making. It also takes what would be a one-sided speech and turns it into a two-way conversation. In addition, asking questions allows you to get more specific information from the speaker, whether you are trying to define a particular point of view, asking about an exact meeting time, or attempting to move the conversation on to a different topic.

Once you have learned how to be an active listener, you will be better able to interpret other people's responses. In doing so, you will naturally become a more effective speaker because your conversation will be a continuous reaction to the responses of the person with whom you are speaking. Whenever you are speaking with someone, however, make sure that your own message gets through in addition to actively listening to the other person's responses and body signals. If necessary, you can modify your message in response to the other person. By paying attention to someone else's message, you invite that person to pay attention to yours. The other person feels heard and respected and will be likely to listen to you and your ideas.

Effective communication is a two-way street. Keeping that pathway open requires both clear communication of your own message and attention to the other person's response. If this sounds like a lot to manage, don't worry—all it takes is some guidance and practice. The payoff will be better relationships and fewer misunderstandings and disagreements with your family, friends, teachers, employers, and coworkers. To help you, use the following suggestions to help you develop habits that can enhance your overall communications skills; speaking is definitely not the only way you can make a statement.

Writing

Effective written communication involves putting your thoughts, opinions, and feelings into writing that other people can read and understand. Written communication can take many forms including short lists of things to do, casual e-mails or text messages, or formal business letters. Although computers have made the mechanical task of writing both faster and easier, logical thinking and clear presentation must come from you.

Good writing skills are an asset in all industries in which people from different divisions of a company work together on projects and communicate regularly by e-mail. In some companies, writing is so important that writing teachers are hired to work with employees, including executives, to improve the quality of their memos, letters, proposals, and reports.

As with most things, to become good at writing, you need to practice. If you would like to improve your writing skills, consider joining the school newspaper or yearbook staff. Try to take classes with teachers who are known to emphasize writing skills, or work with a tutor. Reading is also excellent training. Read a variety of materials, such as newspapers, magazines, books, and Web sites.

Although journal writing is a great way to express the frustrations of stuttering that most people do not understand, it's not a substitute for talking things out.

Personal Writing

Writing a letter to a friend is a fun, expressive way to share an experience. Keep a friendly tone and include a joke, a story, a poem, or a sketch. Remember that there are four formatting requirements that should be followed when writing a letter. The heading at the top right-hand corner

should include your address and the date. A salutation at the beginning is where you greet the person to whom you're writing, using "Dear so-and-so." Write the salutation at the left-hand margin below the heading, and use a comma after the name. The body of the letter includes your thoughts and ideas. Use short paragraphs to hold the reader's attention, and skip one line between paragraphs for easier reading. The letter's closing includes your sign-off and signature and is usually written about two lines below the body.

Journal writing is a form of personal composition that is often kept private, though it can be a great resource for any writer.

Keeping a journal can help a writer maintain his or her focus. Attempt different writing styles in your journal, such as poetry or short stories. Writing in a journal is good practice and can help you become a better writer. Remember to date each entry. When you go back and reread, you can see your progress as well as recall your experiences.

The narrative is probably the most traditional personal writing style. It has a specific format that includes a beginning, middle, and end. The personal narrative is written in the first person (I) and is the retelling of an event using story elements such as setting, character, and plot, or the series of actions that make up your story. Sometimes the word "memoir" is used with this type of writing. A memoir is an autobiographical piece that spans different moments in the author's life. A personal narrative is different from a memoir because it highlights only one specific moment.

Informational Writing

The goal of informational writing is to present the facts surrounding a specific subject in a clear, balanced, and well-researched manner. The writing is objective, meaning it makes clear the facts of a subject, rather than subjective, which presents opinions on the subject. Biographies, classroom essays, reports, and expository pieces are all types of informative writing.

Expository writing is informational writing designed to explain a topic. It often gives facts, explains ideas, or defines conditions with deep insight. With this type of informative

Companies not only look for articulate speakers, but for excellent writers as well. In fact, numerous training programs teach professionals how to become more effective writers.

writing, ideas are presented in a certain order so that the reader can follow the explanation easily. When deciding upon a topic for an expository piece, choose one that you feel can be simply explained.

Biographical writing is informational in that it aims to communicate information about the events in a specific person's life. In a biography, the story normally flows in a chronological order with one moment following another. This information may start at the point of the subject's birth and explain how he or she lived, but it might also begin at a more precise moment.

An informational essay investigates a topic by fully exploring it from all sides, presenting only the facts surrounding the experience. For instance, if you choose to write about your bicycle, you would include factual details such as its color, age, and brand. On the other hand, a report is a much more in-depth investigation of a topic. Informational reports require a solid, well-researched foundation to support the subject. An informational report about your bicycle could even cover the history of your particular make and model.

Persuasive Writing

Persuasive writing introduces an author's strong opinions regarding a specific subject. When you are writing persuasively about something, your goal is to convince the reader that your opinion is relevant. You do this by using language that conveys balanced thoughts, strong convictions, and respect for the reader. When writing persuasively, it is crucial that your thoughts are explained clearly and that your opinions are supported by facts.

Persuasive writing is usually written in the first person ("I think," "I argue," "I support"), and it is frequently written in the present tense. This allows the reader to become involved in the topic, seeing the issue through the author's eyes.

As you think about possible topics, always keep your reader in mind, making sure that you can communicate the importance of your subject to him or her. Address the reader as "you," and treat him or her the way you would a friend with whom you want to share valuable information. By using a confident tone in your writing, which is your personality and author's "voice," you'll convey how strongly you believe in your cause.

Editing Your Work

There are certain traits of good writing that all students must adhere to if they want to sharpen their skills. Following these guidelines will help you polish existing skills to make them more powerful.

- **Concept:** The main idea or topic of your written work is like a tree trunk. It contains all of the nutrients to fortify your story. Its main points are like branches that flow from the concept's base. Informative details can grow like budding leaves from those branches and can take the form of detailed descriptions, anecdotes, quoted or paraphrased information, statistics and other hard data, or just general facts.
- **Order:** The way in which your tree—or concept—grows, or the way it is organized, is equally important as your main idea. While there are many ways to organize your piece

(chronologically, for instance, or by using the inverted triangle method), you must adhere to whatever design you have chosen. Having a good organizational strategy in place will help you make the transitions from point to point more easily.

➤ **Style:** The style of a written work is the author's "voice." You impart this individual style to your writing. Your author's voice is like a personal signature that only you can give your work; it lets the reader know that you are giving something of yourself in your piece that is unique. Your individual author's voice should be evident from the first sentence, or lede, to the last sentence, or conclusion.

➤ **Word choice:** Using precise words to convey specific meanings or emotion in your work is as important as your concept, order, and author's voice. Appropriate words can give your writing power like nothing else can. Always scan your draft to make sure that each word that you have chosen is the best word to express your intended meaning.

➤ **Rhythm:** The flow of sentences in your writing determines if the work has rhythm and momentum. As a rule, you want to vary your sentence length and structure through-out your written work. This means that you should have a mix of both short and long sentences that propel your concept. Always read your work aloud to get a sense of its overall rhythm.

➤ **Mechanics:** The mechanical elements of your writing are the key points that determine if it is correct or not. These elements include spelling, grammar, usage, punctuation, capitalization, and creating solid paragraphs (each with a main point). Always proofread and edit your work line by line while considering all of these conventions separately. Also, an excellent way to check the spelling of each word is to read the work backward from its end to its beginning.

Electronic Communication

It's almost impossible to remember a time when people didn't use some form of electronic instrument for both personal and professional communication. Everywhere you turn, people are writing e-mail, reading text messages, or meeting friends that they met through social networks such as MySpace.com. And while these methods now allow an almost unprecedented and continuous stream of communication, there are certain risks that you should be aware of when using them. Consider the following points:

- When you receive a gift or after a job interview, it is advisable that you thank the person who met with you through the mail, rather than by sending an e-mail message.
- Although communicating on the Internet through social networks and chat rooms is fun, it should never take the place of traditional forms of communication.
- E-mail is informal; it's rarely considered a better form of communication than a written letter sent through the mail or a telephone call.
- You should never divulge your personal information such as your name, address, telephone number, Social Security

FACTS ABOUT
STUTTERING

1 More than 100 muscles are used to produce a single word!

2 A person speaks between 120 and 180 words a minute, during which your vocal tract makes 600 shapes.

3 For every five kids who are born, at least one will stutter.

number, or the location of your school online either in a written profile or when communicating with someone in a chat room or through a social network.

➜ Communicating through e-mail can more easily be misinterpreted than communicating more directly by telephone or in person since the inflections in your voice, as well as your body language, are never revealed in e-mail.

➜ E-mails can be lost, misdirected, or easily deleted.

➜ Many people who you meet online are not who they say they are. They may be falsifying information such as their name, age, gender, location, interest, or motive.

Blogging can give your friends a deeper perspective of your life. However, you should always be aware of who can view your blog and what you write about others in it.

➡ Be advised that any content such as your photograph, profile information, and other facts about you are available to anyone who does a search on the Internet, including potential friends, colleagues, supervisors, employers, and government agencies. Once this information is online, it cannot be changed or retracted.

➡ Be sure to fully read the disclaimer attached to Web sites, social networks such as MySpace.com, or content providers such as YouTube.com. In some cases, you may no longer "own" the information you are uploading. In these instances, your photographs, information, writing, artwork, video, or film is now the property of the company that owns the Web site and can be "resold" without your knowledge or consent.

Sharpening your skills at using other forms of communication can show people that although you stutter, you have compelling, interesting, and intelligent things to say. Moreover, writing skillfully, listening carefully, and being aware of your body language can display exactly how articulate, receptive, and persuasive a communicator you really are.

blocking The act of trying to make a sound that is stopped by a flow of air that is suspended at some point in your body such as your larynx, tongue, or lips.

communication The expression of feelings, ideas, moods, and meanings.

disfluency A disruption in speech; speech that is not smooth.

impulse An electrical message sent from the brain to motivate activity in the body's parts.

larynx A body's voice box found at the top of the trachea; the first place where you make sound by using your vocal folds.

muscle distortion The tensing and contracting of muscles involved in making speech that affects the stutterer when he or she is trying to make sounds.

nonverbal communication The expression of feelings, ideas, moods, and meanings without the aid of speech.

phonation The act or process of making speech.

repetition The act of making a series of the same sounds, syllables, or words.

self-esteem The level of self-worth that a person feels.

speech therapist/speech pathologist A person who is professionally trained to treat speech disorders.

speech therapy Treatment for a speech disorder.

stuck Another term for blocking.

stuttering pattern The individual unique problem each stutterer experiences when he or she is trying to make sounds.

trachea The body's windpipe, which connects the mouth/nose to the bronchi of the lungs.

vocal folds (vocal cords) Muscle flaps in the larynx that open and close and that are responsible for making sounds.

American Institute for Stuttering Treatment and
   Professional Training
27 West 20th Street, Suite 1203
New York, NY 10011
(212) 633-6400
Web site: http://www.stutteringtreatment.org
   This organization provides treatment to children, teens,
   and adults and trains professionals in recognizing and
   treating disfluent speech.

National Institute on Deafness and Other
   Communication Disorders
National Institutes of Health
31 Center Drive, MSC 2320
Bethesda, MD 20892
Web site: http://www.nidcd.nih.gov/health/voice/stutter.asp
   This organization's Web site features a section on voice,
   speech, and language with a specific link to stuttering.

Our Time Theatre Company
307 West 38th Street, Suite 1710
New York, NY 10018
(212) 414-9696
E-mail: moreinfo@ourtimetheatre.org
Web site: http://www.ourtimetheatre.org

Our Time Theatre Company is an organization dedicated to providing an artistic home for young people who stutter. The company members are comprised of young people who stutter who write and perform original plays and music.

Stuttering Foundation of America

3100 Walnut Grove Road, Suite 603

P.O. Box 11749

Memphis, TN 38111-0749

(800) 992-9392

(901) 452-7343

Web site: http://www.stutteringhelp.org
This organization has a hotline on stuttering and a national referral list of speech-language pathologists who specialize in stuttering.

Web Sites

Due to the changing nature of Internet links, Rosen Publishing has developed an online list of Web sites related to the subject of this book. This site is updated regularly. Please use this link to access the list:

http://www.rosenlinks.com/faq/stut

For Further Reading

Fraser, Malcolm. *Self-Therapy for the Stutterer.* Memphis, TN: Stuttering Foundation of America, 2005.

Jezer, Marty. *Stuttering: A Life Bound Up in Words.* Brattleboro, VT: Small Pond Press, 2003.

Lavid, David, M.D. *Understanding Stuttering* (Understanding Health and Sickness). Jackson, MS: University of Mississippi Press, 2004.

Bibliography

Apel, Melanie Ann. *Coping with Stuttering*. New York, NY: Rosen Publishing Group, 2000.

Bobrick, Benson. *Knotted Tongues: Stuttering in History and the Quest for a Cure*. New York, NY: Simon & Schuster, 1995.

Fraser, Malcolm. *Self-Therapy for the Stutterer*. Memphis, TN: Stuttering Foundation of America, 2000.

Ramig, Peter R., and Darrell M. Dodge. *The Child and Adolescent Stuttering Treatment and Activity Resource Guide*. Clifton Park, NY: Thomson Delmar Learning, 2005.

Index

Photo Credits

Designer: Evelyn Horovicz; **Editor:** Roman Espejo
Photo Researcher: Cindy Reiman